The Solar System
태양계

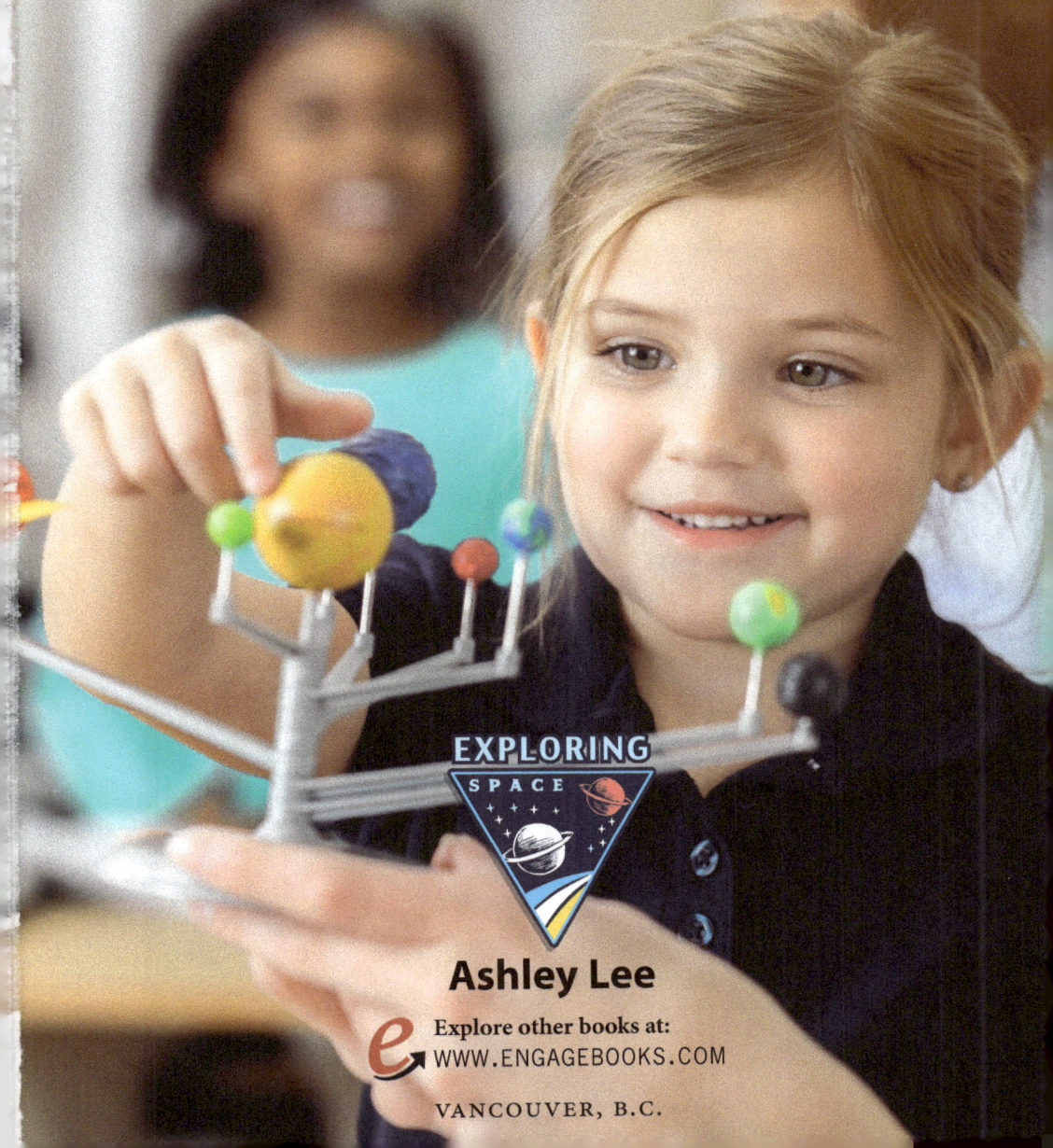

Ashley Lee

Explore other books at:
WWW.ENGAGEBOOKS.COM

VANCOUVER, B.C.

ℰ WWW.ENGAGEBOOKS.COM

The Solar System: Level 1 Bilingual
(English/Korean) (영어/한국어)
Lee, Ashley 1995 —
Text © 2021 Engage Books
Edited by: A.R. Roumanis
and Jared Siemens
Translated by: Gio Oh
Proofread by: Tamara Kazali

Text set in Arial Regular.
Chapter headings set in Arial Black.

FIRST EDITION / FIRST PRINTING

LIBRARY AND ARCHIVES CANADA CATALOGUING IN PUBLICATION

Title: The Solar System Level 1 Bilingual (English/Korean) (영어/한국어)
Names: Lee, Ashley, author.

ISBN 978-1-77476-470-1 (hardcover)
ISBN 978-1-77476-469-5 (softcover)

Subjects:
LCSH: Solar system—Juvenile literature

Classification: LCC QB501.3 .L44 2020 | DDC J523.2—DC23

Contents 목차

What Is the Sun?
태양은 무엇인가요?

The Sun is a star. Stars make light. They are very hot.
태양은 별이에요. 별은 빛을 만들어요. 이들은 매우 뜨겁습니다.

The Sun looks bigger than other stars. It looks bigger because other stars are further away.
태양은 다른 별들보다 커보입니다. 그것은 다른 별들이 더 멀리 떨어져 있기 때문입니다.

What Is the Solar System?
태양계는 무엇인가요?

The Sun is at the center of the solar system.
태양은 태양계의 중심에 있습니다.

All things that move around the
Sun are part of the solar system.
태양주위를 도는 모든 것들은
태양계의 일부입니다.

What Are Planets?
행성은 무엇인가요?

A planet is a round object that moves around a star.
행성은 별 주위를 움직이는 둥근 물체예요.

Venus
금성

Mars
화성

Mercury
수성

Earth
지구

Jupiter
목성

Saturn
토성

Neptune
해왕성

Uranus
천왕성

There are eight planets in the solar system.
태양계에는 총 8개의 행성이 있어요.

What Is Mercury?
수성은 무엇인가요?

Mercury is the smallest planet. It is also the closest planet to the Sun.
화성은 가장 작은 행성이에요. 또한 태양 가장 가까이에있죠.

What Is Venus?
금성은 무엇인가요?

Venus is the hottest planet. It has many mountains and volcanoes.
금성은 가장 뜨거운 행성이에요.
금성에는 산과 화산이 많이 있어요.

11

What Is Earth?
지구는 무엇인가요?

Earth is the only planet in the solar system known to support life. It has oceans that make the planet look blue.

지구는 태양계의 행성중 유일하게 생명체가 사는 행성이에요. 바다가 있기때문에 행성이 파랗게 보여요.

What Is Mars?
화성은 무엇인가요?

Mars is a red planet. Just like Earth, Mars has changing seasons.
화성은 빨간 행성이에요. 지구처럼 화성도 계절의 변화가 있답니다.

What Is Jupiter?
목성은 무엇인가요?

Jupiter is the largest planet.
It has about 80 moons.
목성은 가장 큰 행성이에요.
80개의 달을 가지고 있어요.

What Is Saturn?
토성은 무엇인가요?

Saturn has about seven main groups of rings. These rings are made out of ice and rock.

토성은 약 7개의 주요 고리들을 가지고 있다. 이 고리들은 얼음과 바위로 만들어졌어요.

What Is Uranus?
천왕성은 무엇인가요?

Uranus is the coldest planet. It is called an ice giant because it is mostly made up of ice.
천왕성은 가장 추운 행성이에요. 천왕성은 대부분 얼음으로 이루어져 있기 때문에 얼음 거인이라고도 불려요.

What Is Neptune?
해왕성은 무엇인가요?

Neptune is the furthest planet from the Sun.
해왕성은 태양에서 가장 먼 행성이에요.

The winds on Neptune are some of the strongest in the solar system.
해왕성의 바람은 태양계에서 가장 강력해요.

What are Dwarf Planets?
왜소행성은 무엇인가요?

Dwarf planets are round objects that circle the Sun. They share their space with other objects. The solar system has five known dwarf planets.

왜소행성은 태양주위를 도는 둥근 물체에요. 왜소행성은 다른 물체들과 공간을 공유해요. 태양계에는 5개의 알려진 왜소행성이 있어요.

Haumea spins about six times faster than Earth.
하우메이아는 지구보다 6배 빨리 돌아요.

Ceres is the smallest dwarf planet.
세레스는 가장 작은 왜소행성이에요.

Makemake takes 309 years to travel around the Sun.
마케마케는 태양 주위를 여행하는데 309년이 걸려요.

Eris is the farthest planet from the Sun.
에리스는 태양에서 가장 멀리 떨어져있어요.

Pluto is the largest dwarf planet.
명왕성은 가장 큰 왜소행성이에요.

What Is the Moon?
달은 무엇인가요?

The Moon travels around Earth. The Moon is about four times smaller than Earth.
달은 지구주위를 돌아요.
달은 지구보다 약 4배 정도 작아요.

A spacecraft is needed to get to the Moon. Spacecraft carry people and tools into space.

달에 가려면 우주선이 필요해요. 우주선으로 사람과 도구를 우주로 나릅니다.

What Is an Astronaut?
우주비행사는 무엇인가요?

An astronaut is a person who travels to space.
우주비행사는 우주를 여행하는 사람입니다.

In 1969, Neil Armstrong became the first person to walk on the Moon.
1969년에 닐 암스트롱은 달 위를 걸은 최초의 사람이에요.

Exploring Space
우주 여행하기

People sometimes send robots to explore space. Robots can explore areas of space that are difficult for humans to reach.

사람들은 종종 지구를 탐사하기 위해 로봇을 보내기도 합니다. 로봇은 사람이 닿기 힘든 우주의 여러 곳 까지 탐사 할 수 있습니다.

A robot called *Curiosity* has been exploring Mars since 2012. *Curiosity* is looking for signs of life on Mars.

로봇 큐리오시티는 2012년 이후로 화성을 탐사하고 있습니다. 큐리오시티는 화성에 생명체의 흔적을 찾고 있습니다.

Living on Mars
화성에서 살기

People hope to one day build a city on Mars. Living on Mars would allow scientists to better study the solar system.

사람들은 언젠가 화성에 도시를 짓고 싶어 합니다. 화성에 살면 과학자의 태양계 연구에 도움이 될 것입니다.

Large spacecraft are being built by a company called SpaceX. A trip to Mars would take about 6 months in one of these spacecraft.

스페이스X라는 회사는 큰 우주선을 만들고 있습니다. 화성으로의 여행은 이 우주선들 중 하나로 약 6개월이 걸릴 것입니다.

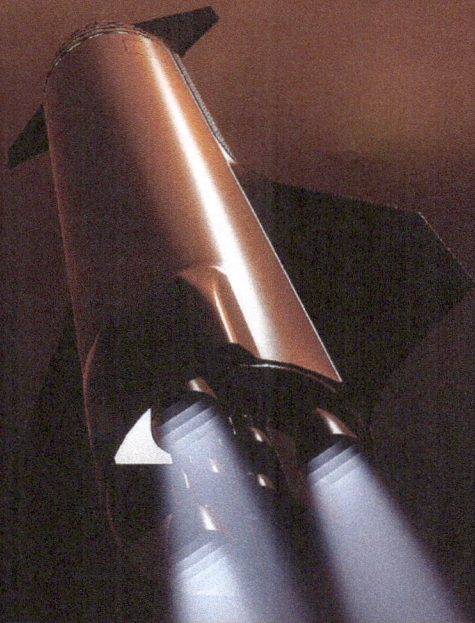

Life Beyond Earth
지구 너머의 삶

Sometimes, animals on Earth become extinct. This means there are no more of them left.

때때로, 지구의 동물들은 멸종합니다. 이것은 단 하나도 남지 않았다라는 뜻이에요.

Exploring space can help humans find new homes. Bringing animals to these places can help make sure that they do not go extinct.

우주를 탐사하는 것은 인간의 새로운 집을 찾는데 도움이 돼요. 그곳에 동물들을 데려가면 동물들이 멸종되지않게 도울 수 있습니다.

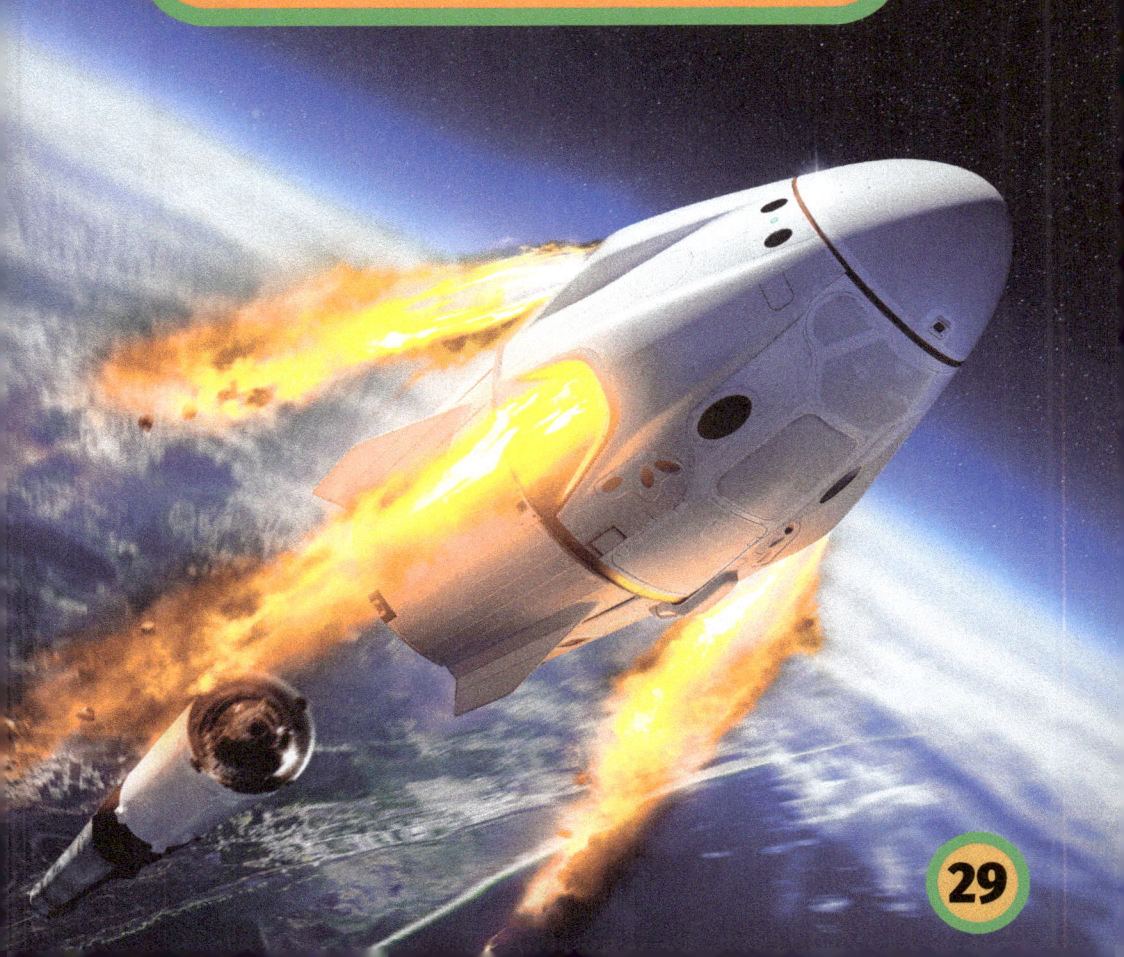

Quiz
퀴즈

Test your knowledge of the solar system by answering the following questions. The questions are based on what you have read in this book. The answers are listed on the bottom of the next page.

아래 질문에 답하면서 태양계에 대한 지식을 테스트 해보세요. 질문은 책의 내용에 기반합니다. 정답은 다음 페이지 밑에 적혀있습니다.

1 What is at the center of the solar system?
태양계 중심에는 무엇이 있나요?

2 What shape are planets?
행성은 무슨 모양인가요?

3 How many planets are in the solar system?
태양계에는 몇개의 행성이 있나요?

4 What is the name of the planet that is closest to the Sun?
태양에 가장 가까운 행성의 이름은 무엇인가요?

5 What is the name of the largest planet in the solar system?
태양계에서 가장 큰 행성의 이름은 무엇인가요?

6 How many known dwarf planets are in the solar system?
태양계에는 몇개의 왜소행성이 있나요?

Explore Other Level 1 Bilingual English/Spanish Readers!

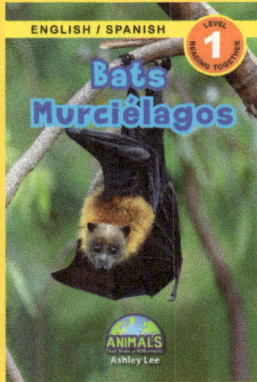

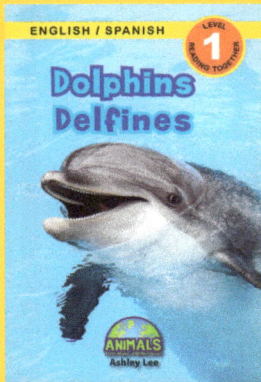

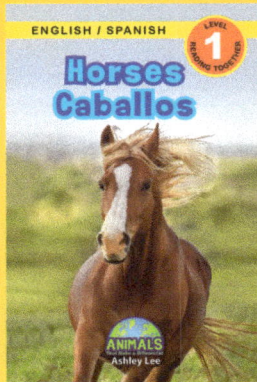

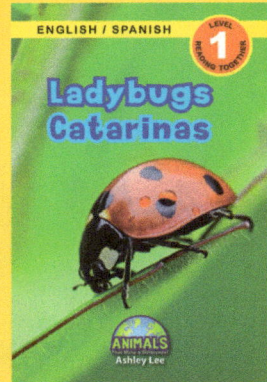

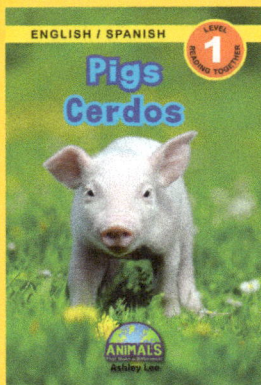

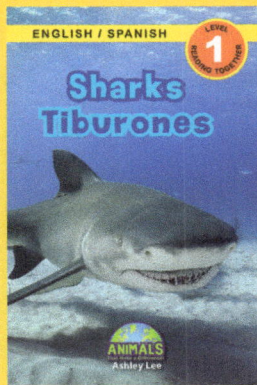

ENGLISH / SPANISH — LEVEL 1 READING TOGETHER
**Bees
Abejas**
ANIMALS
Ashley Lee & Jared Siemens

ENGLISH / SPANISH — LEVEL 1 READING TOGETHER
**Bats
Murciélagos**
ANIMALS
Ashley Lee

ENGLISH / SPANISH — LEVEL 1 READING TOGETHER
**Birds
Aves**
ANIMALS
Ashley Lee

ENGLISH / SPANISH — LEVEL 1 READING TOGETHER
**Dolphins
Delfines**
ANIMALS
Ashley Lee

ENGLISH / SPANISH — LEVEL 1 READING TOGETHER
**Horses
Caballos**
ANIMALS
Ashley Lee

ENGLISH / SPANISH — LEVEL 1 READING TOGETHER
**Ladybugs
Catarinas**
ANIMALS
Ashley Lee

ENGLISH / SPANISH — LEVEL 1 READING TOGETHER
**Pigs
Cerdos**
ANIMALS
Ashley Lee

ENGLISH / SPANISH — LEVEL 1 READING TOGETHER
**Sharks
Tiburones**
ANIMALS
Ashley Lee

ENGLISH / SPANISH — LEVEL 1 READING TOGETHER
**Squirrels
Ardillas**
ANIMALS
Ashley Lee

Visit www.engagebooks.com to explore more Engaging Readers.